INSIDE YOUR BODY

ALL ABOUT HEAD LICE

MEGAN BORGERT-SPANIOL

Consulting Editor, Diane Craig, MA/Reading Specialist

Super Sandcastle

An Imprint of Abdo Publishing
abdopublishing.com

ABDOPUBLISHING.COM

Published by Abdo Publishing, a division of ABDO, PO Box 398166, Minneapolis, Minnesota 55439. Copyright © 2019 by Abdo Consulting Group, Inc. International copyrights reserved in all countries. No part of this book may be reproduced in any form without written permission from the publisher. Super SandCastle™ is a trademark and logo of Abdo Publishing.

Printed in the United States of America,
North Mankato, Minnesota
052018
092018

THIS BOOK CONTAINS
RECYCLED MATERIALS

Design and Production: Mighty Media, Inc.
Editor: Jessie Alkire
Cover Photographs: iStockphoto; Shutterstock
Interior Photographs: iStockphoto; Shutterstock

Library of Congress Control Number: 2017961867

Publisher's Cataloging-in-Publication Data
Names: Borgert-Spaniol, Megan, author.
Title: All about head lice / by Megan Borgert-Spaniol.
Description: Minneapolis, Minnesota : Abdo Publishing, 2019. |
     Series: Inside your body set 2
Identifiers: ISBN 9781532115813 (lib.bdg.) | ISBN 9781532156533
     (ebook)
Subjects: LCSH: Human body--Juvenile literature. | Head lice
     infestation--Juvenile literature. | Host-parasite relationships--
     Juvenile literature. | Communicable diseases--Juvenile literature.
Classification: DDC 616.57--dc23

Super SandCastle™ books are created by a team of professional educators, reading specialists, and content developers around five essential components—phonemic awareness, phonics, vocabulary, text comprehension, and fluency—to assist young readers as they develop reading skills and strategies and increase their general knowledge. All books are written, reviewed, and leveled for guided reading, early reading intervention, and Accelerated Reader™ programs for use in shared, guided, and independent reading and writing activities to support a balanced approach to literacy instruction.

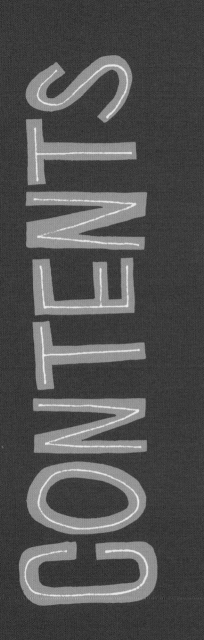

CONTENTS

YOUR BODY

AREA MOST AFFECTED BY HEAD LICE

You're amazing! So is your body.
Most of the time your body works just fine.
It lets you go to school, play with friends,
and more. But sometimes you feel sick or
part of you hurts.

Millions of kids get head lice each year. Head lice won't hurt you. But they make your head **itch**. And sometimes they are hard to get rid of! An adult or doctor can help treat your head lice!

ALL ABOUT
HEAD
LICE

Head lice are tiny insects. They are parasites. They feed on small amounts of human blood. Lice need human blood to stay alive.

Head lice live on people's **scalps**. This is because the scalp is warm. It also has hair. Head lice grab onto the hair of the scalp. They also lay eggs in the hair.

PARASITE
(PAIR-uh-site)

. . . .

a living thing that feeds
on another living thing
to stay alive

Louse is the word for
one of the lice.

CAUSES

Head lice spread through head contact. Lice can also spread when people share hats, brushes, pillows, and other items that touch hair.

Anyone can get head lice. But kids are the most likely to get it. This is because they often come in close contact with one another. This happens in school, sports, or at sleepovers.

Clean or Dirty?

Some people think having lice is a sign of being unclean. This isn't true. It doesn't matter how clean your hair is! Lice can live on anyone.

No Touch, No Problem

Lice cannot jump or fly. You won't catch head lice just by sitting near someone with head lice.

Pet Lice

Dogs and cats can get lice. But their lice won't spread to humans. And pets cannot catch human lice!

THE LIFE OF A
LOUSE

Once a louse finds a head to live on, it lays eggs. Then the eggs hatch into more lice. Lice can live up to four weeks on a person's head. They go through three stages.

Nits

Lice lay eggs called nits in the hair. Lice attach their eggs to the root of the hair near the **scalp**. Heat from the scalp keeps the eggs warm until they hatch.

Nymphs

Lice nits hatch after one or two weeks. Baby lice are called nymphs.

Adults

Nymphs become adults a week or two after hatching. Then they start to lay eggs. Adults can lay up to eight eggs a day!

SIGNS

AND SYMPTOMS

Itching is the main **symptom** of head lice. Do you have a tickling feeling on your **scalp**? Are you scratching your head often? If so, tell an adult right away. He or she can help you look for signs of lice.

Nits

Nits that haven't hatched yet look like yellowish brown ovals. Hatched nits are white or clear. Nits are attached to strands of hair. They don't come off hair easily.

Adult Lice

A louse is gray or tan. It is about the size of a sesame seed. You might see a louse crawling in your hair. But you are more likely to see nits.

Red Bumps

Look for red bumps on your **scalp**, neck, and shoulders. These spots show where lice have bitten.

TREATMENT

A case of head lice should be treated right away. Otherwise, the lice will continue to hatch, grow, and lay eggs.

Your doctor can help you decide how to treat your head lice. **Treatment** often includes washing and combing the lice from your hair.

Washing

Wash your hair with a medicated shampoo or cream. These kill lice and nits. You can get these products at a drugstore. Or, your doctor might **prescribe** one for you.

Combing

Have an adult remove the lice and nits from your wet hair. This should be done with a fine-tooth comb. Do this once every three or four days for at least two weeks.

Warning!

Shampoos and creams that treat head lice have strong chemicals in them. Do not use more than you are supposed to. This could harm your skin.

If you have lice, other people in your home might too. It's a good idea to check and treat everyone at once!

INFECTION!

Your **scalp** may continue to **itch** for a few days after **treatment**. But try not to scratch too much. Doing so can tear your skin and let bacteria in. This causes an **infection**.

A scalp infection may need to be treated with antibiotics. Call your doctor if you start to notice signs of a scalp infection!

RED, TENDER SKIN

SORES THAT OOZE AND CRUST OVER

SWOLLEN LYMPH GLANDS IN NECK

Itching!

Why do head lice make your head **itch** so much? A louse bites your **scalp** to drink small amounts of blood. The itching is your body's **reaction** to the louse's **saliva**!

EVERY LAST
LOUSE

Treatment should get rid of the lice on your head. But your pillows, sheets, and more could still be **infested** with lice. It is important to clean everything your head may have touched.

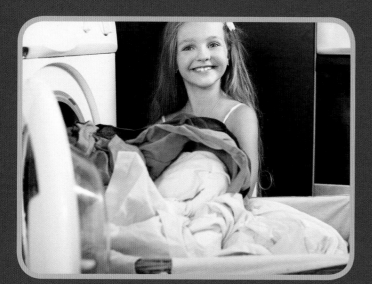

WASH BED SHEETS AND CLOTHING IN VERY HOT WATER.

VACUUM ALL CARPETS AND FURNITURE IN YOUR HOME.

CLEAN COMBS AND BRUSHES WITH
HOT WATER OR RUBBING ALCOHOL.

PLACE PILLOWS AND STUFFED
ANIMALS IN AN AIRTIGHT BAG
FOR TWO WEEKS.

GOING TO THE
DOCTOR

Sometimes head lice don't go away after **treatment**. This can happen for several reasons.

- Some nits were left on the hair after treatment. The nits then hatched into more lice.

- A friend or classmate is still spreading head lice.

- Pillows, brushes, or other items were not properly washed.

- The medicated shampoo or cream did not kill the lice.

I still have head lice two weeks after treatment. What should I do?

DO NOT use the same medicated shampoo or cream more than three times.

DO call your doctor. She might suggest a stronger shampoo or a medicine you can take by mouth.

PREVENTION

Head lice can spread quickly. Even kids who stay clean and healthy get it! But you can still try to keep lice out of your hair.

BRING YOUR OWN PILLOW AND BLANKETS TO SLEEPOVERS.

DO NOT SHARE CLOTHING OR HAIR ITEMS WITH FRIENDS. THESE INCLUDE HATS, SCARVES, BRUSHES, AND HAIR CLIPS.

AVOID STORING COATS OR HATS IN
SHARED SPACES SUCH AS CLOSETS
AND LOCKERS.

AVOID HEAD-TO-HEAD CONTACT
WITH ANYONE WHO HAS LICE.

IF SOMEONE AT SCHOOL HAS
HEAD LICE, HAVE AN ADULT
CHECK YOUR HAIR!

GLOSSARY

INFECTION – an unhealthy condition caused by bacteria or other germs.

INFESTED – spreading or existing in large numbers so as to cause trouble or harm.

ITCH – to feel irritated or bothersome.

PRESCRIBE – to order the use of a medicine or treatment.

REACTION – a response to a stimulus.

SALIVA – a liquid produced in the mouth.

SCALP – the part of the human head usually covered with hair.

SYMPTOM – a noticeable change in the normal working of the body.

TREATMENT – medical or surgical care for a sickness or an injury.